READ ABOUT

Mammals

Anna Claybourne

COPPER BEECH BOOKS

BROOKFIELD, CONNECTICUT

Contents

1 What Are Mammals?   **page 3**
What Makes a Mammal? • Types of Mammals

2 Mammals at Home   **page 8**
Habitats • Burrows and Other Homes

3 Finding Food   **page 16**
Meat- and Plant-Eaters • Hunting • Omnivores

4 Having Babies   **page 22**
How Babies Are Born • Mammal Eggs • Names

5 Can Mammals Talk?   **page 27**
Sending Messages • Teaching Mammals to Talk

Find Out More   **page 30**

Index and Picture Answers   **page 32**

© Aladdin Books Ltd 2000

Designed and produced by
Aladdin Books Ltd
28 Percy Street
London W1P 0LD

First published in
the United States in 2000 by
Copper Beech Books,
an imprint of
The Millbrook Press
2 Old New Milford Road
Brookfield, Connecticut 06804

ISBN 0-7613-1213-7
Cataloging-in-Publication data is on file
at the Library of Congress.

Printed in U.A.E.

All rights reserved

Editor
Jim Pipe

Science Consultant
David Burnie

Series Literacy Consultant
Wendy Cobb

Design
Flick, Book Design and Graphics

Picture Research
Brooks Krikler Research

What Are Mammals?

A mammal is a kind of animal. There are lots of different kinds, from tiny mice to lions and tigers, big elephants, and blue whales. But what makes them all mammals?

The polar bear is a mammal.

First of all, mammals look after their babies when they are born. That might not sound strange to you — but that's because you're a mammal, too!

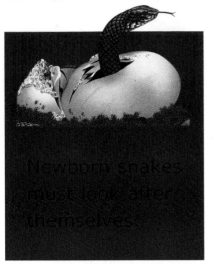

Newborn snakes must look after themselves.

In fact, lots of animals don't care for their babies. Many insects and fish don't even see their babies. The adults die or leave before their eggs hatch.

Mammals always care for their young. A mother mammal stays with her babies, keeps them warm, and feeds them on special milk from her body.

A mother wolf feeds milk to her cubs.

There are other ways to spot a mammal:

• All mammals have hair, fur, or prickly spines. Think of a horse's mane, a furry rabbit, and the spikes on a hedgehog. Even a whale has a few hairs near its mouth.

• Mammals are warm-blooded. This means their body can keep warm even when it's cold outside. So they can live in all sorts of places.

• Mammals are clever! They have a bigger brain and learn more quickly than other animals.

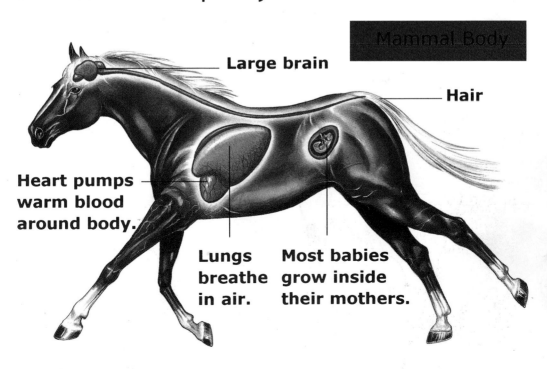

Mammal Body

Large brain

Hair

Heart pumps warm blood around body.

Lungs breathe in air.

Most babies grow inside their mothers.

Birds, fish, reptiles, and insects aren't mammals. So which animals are mammals? There are over 4,600 different types. They include some of the biggest and brainiest animals in the world.

1 Four-legged animals like tigers, dogs, mice, horses, and zebras.

2 Strange-looking creatures like pangolins, sloths, and kangaroos.

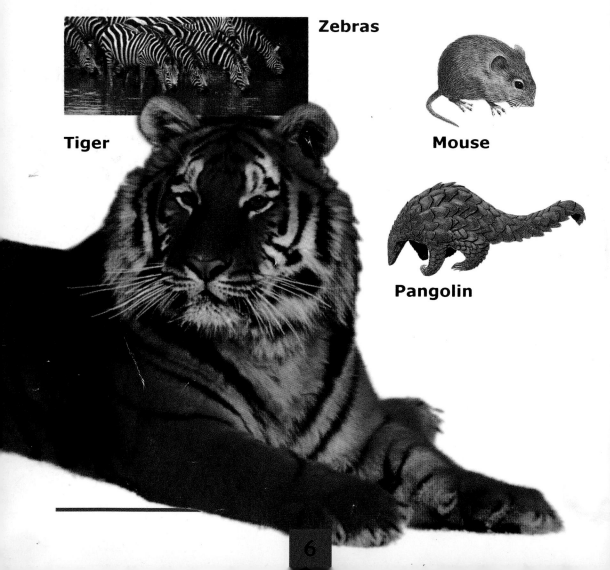

Zebras

Tiger

Mouse

Pangolin

Below are some of the main types of mammal. Don't forget that humans are mammals as well. Perhaps that's why so many people like mammals — because they're a bit like us.

3 Big sea animals like whales and dolphins (but not sharks, which are fish).

Whales

Spider monkey

Bat

4 Bats, the only mammals that can really fly.

5 Animals with arms and legs, like monkeys, chimpanzees, and people.

Mammals at Home

There are mammals in every part of the world. They live in jungles and on grasslands, up high mountains, in hot deserts, and even in seas.

Not all mammals can survive in all these places. A whale can't live up a tree, and a monkey wouldn't last very long in the middle of the Pacific Ocean.

Each mammal has changed, or adapted, over millions of years so it fits the place it lives in — its habitat.

Do you know what sort of place gorillas are adapted for? Answer on page 32.

8

A baby harp seal can lie in the snow without freezing.

Mammals that live in cold places may have lots of extra-thick, soft fur. Or they may have a layer of fat, called blubber, under their skin. It acts like a blanket to keep them warm.

Harp seals can stay warm in the snow and freezing water around the Arctic Circle. They have both fur and blubber to keep out the cold.

A camel can drink sixteen gallons (sixty liters) of water at once. Then it can go for over a week without another drink.

But what about mammals that live in hot, dry places? Well, they've adapted, too.

Camels live in the desert. It is *very* hot and they have short fur to keep the sun from burning their skin. They have thick pads on their feet so that the burning sand doesn't hurt them.

Mammals that live in the jungle need a good grip so they can swing from branch to branch (below). That's why apes and monkeys have rubbery hands with long fingers and thumbs.

All mammals have to breathe air, even if they live in the sea. They can't breathe underwater like fish.

Sea mammals like seals and dolphins are very good at holding their breath. They go for a swim, then come to the surface to breathe.

A whale breathes through a hole in the top of its head.

A mole's big, tough claws are shaped for digging.

Many mammals make themselves a home to live in. Most of them dig a hole or burrow in the ground.

Some mammals, like moles and gerbils, live alone in their hole.

Other mammals, like rabbits, live in a big group called a colony. They share a network of tunnels all joined together.

Thousands of prairie dogs live together in burrows under the ground.

Instead of digging holes, beavers build themselves a home, called a lodge, out of mud, sticks, and stones.

Beavers are good swimmers. They build their lodge in a river or lake so that the entrances are underwater. That way, their home is safe from bears and wolves.

How does a beaver cut down trees to make its home? Answer on page 32.

Bats hang from tree branches or from the roof of a cave. They even sleep upside down!

Cougars and snow leopards often make a den in a cave. They use it to rest in during the day, and to have their babies in.

Lots of mammals don't have a home at all. Some just sleep on their feet, like horses, goats, and antelopes.

In cold countries, some mammals spend all winter asleep in their home (above). They don't eat, but live off the fat stored in their body. We call this "hibernating."

Finding Food

Meat- and Plant-Eaters • Hunting • Omnivores

The flying fox, a type of large bat, eats fruit and flowers.

Like all animals, mammals eat either meat or plants, or both.

Plant-eaters are called herbivores. Some eat leaves and stalks, some eat roots and seeds, some eat fruit, and some eat flowers, bark, or wood.

Giraffes, horses, sheep, and cows are all plant-eating mammals.

Another herbivore is the pika. This small, furry mammal eats plants like grass and twigs.

Pikas live on mountains in Asia and North America. It's very cold here in winter, and not many plants can grow. So every fall, each pika gathers a large pile of plants and dries them in the sun. This store of food lasts all winter.

Like many herbivores, pikas have sharp eyesight and hearing. They are good at watching out for other animals who might want to eat them.

A pika calls out to warn of danger.

Mammal hunters can be small. A 4-inch hedgehog eats insects, snakes, other mammals, and birds.

Meat-eaters are called carnivores. They hunt and kill other animals to eat. Big cats, wolves, seals, and anteaters are all carnivores.

The tiger is a meat-eater. It's very big, but its stripes make it hard to see in the long grass. It is also very good at hiding and creeping up on other animals.

The tiger suddenly pounces and grabs its prey with its claws. Tigers are very strong — they can kill animals much bigger than themselves.

Tigers aren't always lucky enough to catch food every day. So when they do kill an animal, they fill themselves up. They eat every bit of the meat and sometimes the bones as well.

This tiger has caught a small deer in a forest in India.

Tamarins eat insects, small birds, and fruits. They are part of the monkey family.

Animals that eat both plants and meat are called omnivores, which means "everything-eaters." Badgers, bears, and some kinds of monkeys are omnivores.

Grizzly bears live in the mountains of Canada. The food they find changes throughout the year, so they eat whatever they can get.

In spring, there are plenty of green shoots and leaves to eat. Bears also steal eggs laid by birds, and catch small mammals such as mice.

In summer, salmon swim up streams and rivers to breed. So the bears go fishing! They jump into the water and grab salmon in their paws.

In the fall, the bears have a feast of fruit, nuts, and berries before hibernating through winter. They also like eating honey, which they find in bees' nests.

Which kind of mammal are you? Humans are usually omnivores. But if you eat only nuts, fruit, and vegetables, you're a herbivore.

What are these bears doing? Answer on page 32.

Having Babies

How Babies Are Born • Mammal Eggs • Names

Most mammals are born in the same way. Let's look at baby elephants to see what happens.

Most of the time, female elephants stay together in a group. But sometimes male elephants join them, looking for a mate.

After they mate, the female elephant gets pregnant. A baby starts to grow inside her body. When it's ready to come out, the baby is born.

Male elephants stay with females for just a few days while they are mating.

If a baby elephant is in danger, the grown-ups protect it by standing around it in a ring.

When it is born, the baby is much smaller than its parents. It can't look after itself and drinks its mother's milk for about six months. Then it begins to eat leaves and roots as well.

All the females in the group babysit for each other. They nudge the babies along with their trunks and keep them out of trouble.

This cheetah is teaching her cubs to hunt. She has caught an antelope.

As baby mammals get older, they learn to find their own food. They grow bigger and stronger until they can look after themselves.

When baby kangaroos and koalas are born, they are too tiny to survive outside. Instead, they crawl into a cozy pouch on their mother's tummy.

A baby kangaroo, called a joey, peers out of its mother's pouch.

Inside the pouch, the babies drink their mother's milk until they grow big enough to come out. If there is danger, they jump back in!

Do mammals lay eggs? Hardly ever. There are just two kinds of mammals that lay eggs — platypuses and echidnas (say "platt-i-pusses" and "i-kid-nas").

Platypus

Platypuses are river mammals. A mother platypus lays her eggs in a riverside burrow and stays with them to keep them warm.

Echidna

After about ten days, the eggs hatch. Then the babies feed on their mother's milk.

A mouse and her young

Like us, most mammals only have one or two babies at a time. But some mammals have more. A mouse can have twelve babies!

Different kinds of baby mammals have different names. Here are some of them.

Elephant — Calf   **Seal — Pup**   **Fox — Kit**

Hare — Leveret   **Bear — Cub**   **Zebra — Foal**

Can Mammals Talk?

Sending Messages • Teaching Mammals to Talk

We humans are the only mammals that can speak in sentences. Other mammals use movements, noises, and smells to send each other messages.

Lots of mammals, such as cats and foxes, have their own area. This is called their territory. They leave smelly droppings around to tell other animals where it is — and to keep away.

A wolf howls to send a message a long way. Close up, it makes faces and moves its body.

Dolphins squeak and whistle to each other as they swim along. If a dolphin is lost or hurt, it cries out. When other dolphins hear the cry, they go to help.

When a dolphin is ill, or having a baby, other dolphins help by holding it up with their flippers.

Like many clever mammals, dolphins enjoy playing games with each other.

When scientists try to teach animals to talk, they usually use mammals like dolphins, gorillas, or chimpanzees. They are among the cleverest animals.

Mammals can't speak, so they have to learn to press buttons with symbols on them. Each button means a different word.

One day, we might be able to talk to the other mammals and find out what it's really like to be one of them!

Some chimps and gorillas talk with their hands to their human friends.

Some have learned hundreds of different words.

Find Out More

PICTURE QUIZ

Do you know which of the following animals are mammals and which aren't? If you need help, turn to pages 6-7 for some clues. The answers are on page 32.

a

b

c

d

e

f

UNUSUAL WORDS

Here we explain some difficult words you will find in this book.

Adapt If animals have adapted, it means their body has changed over millions of years so they are suited to their habitat.

Blubber A thick layer of fat under the skin.

Carnivore An animal that eats only meat.

Colony A group of animals, such as rabbits, that live together.

Habitat The kind of place an animal lives in, such as a desert.

Herbivore An animal that eats only plants.

Hibernation Saving energy by sleeping through winter.

Omnivore An animal that eats both plants and other animals.

Reptile A scaly animal that lays eggs. Lizards, crocodiles, snakes, and tortoises are reptiles.

Territory The area an animal lives in and marks out for itself.

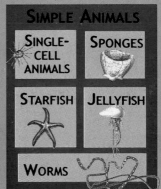

RECORD BREAKERS
Biggest Mammal
The blue whale is the biggest animal in the world. It can weigh over two hundred tons and can grow as long as five buses.

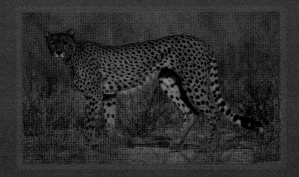

Fastest Mammal
The fastest mammal is the cheetah. For a short time, a cheetah can run at nearly seventy miles per hour.

THE ANIMAL KINGDOM
Scientists have put animals into groups to show how they are related. Mammals are closest to birds and reptiles.

ANIMALS WITH BACKBONES

Mammals	Birds	Reptiles	Amphibians	Fish

ANIMALS WITHOUT BACKBONES

MOLLUSKS

Snails	Clams	Octopuses

ARTHROPODS

Spiders	Insects	Crustaceans

SIMPLE ANIMALS

SINGLE-CELL ANIMALS	SPONGES
STARFISH	JELLYFISH
WORMS	

Index

Anteaters 18
Antelopes 15, 24
Apes 10

Babies 3-4, 15, 22-26
Badgers 20
Bats 7, 14, 16
Bears 3, 13, 20, 21, 26
Beavers 13
Birds 6, 18, 20

Camels 10
Carnivores 18, 30
Cats 18, 27
Cheetahs 24, 31
Chimpanzees 7, 29
Colonies 12, 30
Cougars 15
Cows 16

Dogs 6
Dolphins 7, 11, 28, 29

Echidnas 25
Eggs 4, 20, 25
Elephants 3, 22, 23, 26

Fish 4, 6, 7, 11
Flying fox 16
Fox 26, 27

Gerbils 12
Giraffes 16
Goats 15
Gorillas 8, 29

Habitats 8-12, 30
Hedgehog 5, 18
Herbivores 16-17, 21, 30
Hibernation 15, 21, 30
Horses 5, 6, 15, 16
Humans 7, 21, 27

Insects 4, 6, 18, 20

Kangaroos 6, 24
Koalas 24

Lions 3

Mice 3, 6, 20, 26
Moles 12
Monkeys 7, 8, 10, 20

Omnivores 20, 21, 30

Pangolins 6
Pikas 17
Platypuses 25
Polar bears 3
Prairie dogs 12

Rabbits 5, 12
Reptiles 6, 30

Seals 9, 11, 26
Sheep 16
Snakes 4, 18
Sloths 6
Snow leopards 15

Tamarins 20
Territories 27, 30
Tigers 3, 6, 18, 19

Whales 3, 5, 7, 8, 11, 31
Wolves 4, 13, 18, 27

Zebras 6, 26

ANSWERS TO PICTURE QUESTIONS

Page 8 Gorillas are adapted for life in the jungle. They have long arms for climbing trees.

Page 13 Beavers use their long, sharp teeth to cut the wood.

Page 21 The bears are fishing for salmon with their big paws.

Page 30 a is a bird, which is not a mammal; b is a dolphin, which is a mammal; c is a frog, which is an amphibian; d is a hippopotamus, another mammal; e is a bee, which is an insect; f is a raccoon, also a mammal.

Photocredits: Abbreviations: t-top, m-middle, b-bottom, r-right, l-left, c-center.
Cover & pages 13, 19 & 29—Planet Earth Pictures. 1, 6 both, 7, 8, 9, 11t, 14, 16, 23, 24b & 28—Digital Stock. 3, 15, 24t & 27—Oxford Scientific Films. 11b & 17—Bruce Coleman Collection.
Illustrators: Richard Orr, Rob Shone, Myke Taylor, Peter Barrett, Shireen Faircloth, Chris Shields.